Neuro-Ethical Realism:

When Biology Becomes Morality

Sofia Derin

A philosophical continuation of her memoir *Trial by Trust*, exploring the body as conscience, and biology as the foundation of truth.

Dedication

For Stallion - my universe, my conscience, and my biology.

You came into my life after I had already lived half of it, yet you walked beside me as I became the proof - as *Trial by Trust* turned life into data and *Neuro-Ethical Realism* turned survival into meaning. This work exists because you reminded me that truth, once lived, never dies; it simply evolves.

Disclaimer

This book explores trauma, morality, and human behaviour through a philosophical and biological lens. While inspired by lived experience, all interpretations are reflective, not prescriptive.

Neuro-Ethical Realism presents the author's independent perspective on conscience and biology. It is not a substitute for psychological, legal, or medical advice, nor does it represent the views of any religion or institution.

All events drawn from the memoir *Trial by Trust* have been reinterpreted here for philosophical illustration. Where names or identifying details appear, they may have been changed to preserve privacy.

Preface

From Survival to System: The Birth of Neuro-Ethical Realism

There comes a point when reflection turns into structure.

When you have told the story of your life enough times to realize that every pattern, every decision, every silence was following its own logic, a logic of biology, conscience, and survival.

Trial by Trust was that story.

It was my anatomy of experience, a dissection of what it means to trust, break, rebuild, and keep breathing. But what came after the last page was something else entirely - *understanding*.

I began to see that conscience doesn't appear in courtrooms, classrooms, or pulpits first. It appears in the body - in the tremor before we speak, in the pulse that tightens when we sense deception, in the relief that follows truth.

We don't learn morality; we feel it, and when we ignore those signals long enough, the body keeps score until it finally speaks louder than our conditioning.

That observation became a framework - a lived theory I call *Neuro-Ethical Realism*. It's the recognition that ethics are not abstract ideals floating above us; they are neurological responses within us.

Morality is a biological rhythm that can be suppressed by fear, amplified by freedom, and rewritten through coherence.

Every page that follows is built from that principle.

Where *Trial by Trust* asked, "What happened to me?", this book asks, "What does that teach us about being human?"

It explores how trauma distorts moral intuition, how culture disguises obedience as virtue, and how autonomy is reclaimed not through ideology, but through re-embodiment.

You don't need to agree with me; you only need to notice how your body reacts as you read. If something tightens, that's your conscience speaking. If something exhales, that's truth finding room to live again.

This is not a self-help manual or a revenge diary. It is the field notes of someone who finally learned that ethics and biology share a heartbeat, that to heal the mind, you must first trust the body.

Welcome to Neuro-Ethical Realism - where survival becomes philosophy, and philosophy finally becomes human.

The Manifesto of Neuro-Ethical Realism

This book was born from the same marrow that wrote *Trial by Trust*. It came from the nights when I couldn't sleep because the body remembered what the mind wanted to forget, when morality wasn't a word but a pulse.

People often say time heals everything. I've learned it doesn't. Time gives you distance, not understanding. Only truth heals, and truth doesn't come from books or beliefs. It comes from biology.

I didn't invent Neuro-Ethical Realism sitting at a desk with theories. It emerged while trying to survive, in the moment my nervous system learned to recognize lies faster than my mind could translate them. It came from shaking hands while signing affidavits, from chest tightness during court hearings, from the surge of clarity that followed fear.

At some point I realized:

The body is the conscience.

Everything else, culture, religion, law, is commentary.

Neuro-Ethical Realism is the understanding that morality begins as a sensory truth. We feel injustice before we can define it. We know danger before it's spoken, and we collapse not from weakness, but from contradiction, when what we feel doesn't match what we're told.

To live by this realism is to reunite the body with its authority. It means trusting your pulse over dogma, your instincts over tradition, and your silence only when it's chosen, not imposed.

The world is full of systems built by people who forgot how to feel; courts that can't sense distress, religions that call obedience virtue, governments that treat trauma like inconvenience. We cannot fix these structures with logic alone. Empathy must become policy. Conscience must be measurable not by creed, but by conduct.

When we design systems that ignore the body, we end up criminalizing emotion and glorifying control. That's not civilization, that's pathology disguised as order.

The Core Principles

1. Morality is biological.

Your nervous system detects truth before your intellect names it.

2. Conscience is measurable.

It can be observed in behaviour - empathy, accountability, repair.

3. Healing is ethical recalibration.

To recover is to bring your biology and beliefs into coherence.

4. Autonomy is sacred.

No ideology, government, or partner owns your moral compass.

5. Justice without empathy is violence.

Systems that do not feel, fail.

Trial by Trust was my evidence.

Neuro-Ethical Realism is my conclusion.

I wrote the memoir to show what happens when conscience is punished. I wrote this to prove that the same biology that breaks can also rebuild truth. This philosophy isn't about perfection, it's about coherence.

It asks one question:

Does your body agree with your choices?

If not, the answer isn't in heaven or in law, it's inside you.

If you've ever been told you're too emotional, too sensitive, too much, this book is your permission slip to be accurate instead, because emotion isn't excess; it's evidence. Feeling deeply is not weakness; it's advanced moral intelligence.

We are not here to be forgiven for surviving.

We are here to redefine what surviving means.

I am no longer writing for validation. I'm writing for verification, that biology and morality are not enemies but allies, that conscience is not divine punishment but human evolution, and if the world insists on dividing us by faith, gender, or title, let me stand as proof that one nervous system - scarred, honest, unafraid - can still become philosophy.

I am Sofia Derin.

I am human data.

I am the theory I was searching for.

Table of Contents

CHAPTER 1

The Body of Conscience

You know when something feels wrong before you can explain why? That tightening in your gut, the sting behind your eyes, the sudden silence that floods your chest.

That's conscience. Not a voice from heaven, not a moral checklist, but a biological alarm system built into the human body.

We like to think morality is taught - that it's a matter of good parenting, religion, or education. But before a child learns a single rule, they feel. They flinch at unfairness. They reach to comfort. They withdraw from cruelty. Their body responds before their mind has the language for it.

Conscience begins in the flesh. It's the body's way of saying, "This doesn't align."

The First Language of Morality

Before words, before reasoning, before fear of punishment, there is the pulse.

The body senses danger and deceit in real time. You can see it in a toddler who hides behind a parent when a stranger's tone changes, or in the child who feels guilty for something no one has accused them of yet. Their body is already fluent in right and wrong.

I remember those sensations long before I understood what adults meant by "right" and "wrong."

My chest would tighten around certain people. I could sense deceit before I could define it. It wasn't supernatural, it was neurological. My body detected threats in micro-expressions, vocal tones, pauses.

People said I was "too sensitive." But sensitivity isn't fragility, it's data. It's the nervous system scanning for coherence, and coherence, that invisible harmony between what someone says, does, and feels, is the deepest human craving. We don't need religion to tell us to value truth; our biology aches for it.

That's the first pillar of Neuro-Ethical Realism: morality doesn't descend from law or religion. It rises from physiology - from the nervous system, the gut, the pulse. The body is the first courtroom, and the heart is its witness.

When We Betray the Body

When we ignore our truth, our body protests - tight shoulders, sleepless nights, grinding teeth, migraines. People call it stress, but often it's the cost of self-betrayal. We live in a world that teaches suppression as strength. Children are told to "be polite," "forgive," "don't make a scene." We learn to perform morality instead of feeling it.

That's when the body starts keeping score.

Every time we override that inner tightening; when we smile through disrespect, stay quiet through injustice, or pretend we're fine when we're not, we dull the biological signal of conscience. The body whispers don't, and the mind says I must.

Over time, we forget how to listen altogether.

Religious morality teaches fear of punishment, social morality teaches fear of judgement, but biological morality – conscience, teaches alignment.

It tells us peace feels better than chaos, truth feels lighter than deceit. That's not a moral opinion, that's neuroscience.

Shame: The Corruption of Conscience

Here's where it gets tricky: the body doesn't only record truth, it also records shame.

When conscience meets trauma, the signal scrambles. Children who grow up around gaslighting or emotional manipulation start to confuse fear with wrongdoing. They feel guilty not because they did something immoral, but because their safety once depended on compliance. This is how entire societies build moral codes that have nothing to do with real ethics.

We mistake obedience for virtue.

We confuse shame with morality.

And the more disconnected we are from our own bodies, the easier we are to control.

The first moral injury most people ever suffer is not a crime, it's silence. The moment they feel something's wrong, but no one believes them. The body warns them, but culture tells them to stay quiet. That's when the split begins, the fracture between conscience and conditioning.

The Biological Cost of Lying to Ourselves

You can lie to anyone except your nervous system.

It knows.

It reacts.

It manifests through fatigue, inflammation, anxiety, depression - all symptoms of an organism forced to live in contradiction. People who say they "don't believe in intuition" are usually people who stopped trusting their own body long ago. They learned to fear the truth because truth often meant loss - loss of belonging, of approval, of control.

But denying truth doesn't erase it. It just gets buried deeper, beneath tension, illness, or endless distraction.

The body becomes a storage unit for everything the mind refuses to face, and that's why healing, true healing, always begins with coherence.

Coherence isn't comfort, it's truth without resistance. It's when your values, actions, and words align so tightly that your nervous system finally relaxes. That's what peace really is, not silence, not stillness, but the absence of inner conflict.

How We Lost the Body's Wisdom

At some point, civilization decided that morality had to come from outside the human being. It was too dangerous to let people trust themselves, so religion, culture, and hierarchy took over. They replaced biological conscience with man-made commandments. Instead of "listen to your body," they said, "obey the rules." and obedience became the enemy of integrity.

We forgot that conscience isn't learned, it's inherited through evolution. Empathy, fairness, reciprocity, these are survival traits. The species that co-operates survive longer than the one that deceives itself. But because we live in systems built on hierarchy, we were taught to suppress the very instincts that make us humane.

We moralized submission. We spiritualized guilt, and in doing so, we disconnected from the instrument that never lies: the body.

The Return to Inner Ethics

To reclaim our conscience, we must return to embodiment, not as spiritual practice, but as a biological necessity - sit still long enough, and you'll feel the truth pulse through your skin.

Your conscience doesn't need language, only permission.

When you learn to read your body again, you rediscover a guidance system far older than scripture.

That's the foundation of Neuro-Ethical Realism:

Morality isn't a belief system; it's a sensory system.

It's the sum of millions of years of biological evolution, designed to keep us coherent within ourselves and connected to others. Religion hijacked it. Society rewired it. But the signal still lives inside you, and that signal, that instinctive recognition of alignment, is where this philosophy begins.

Because before ethics became theory, before religion became power, before society taught us to perform good instead of living it - the body already knew.

CHAPTER 2

The Hijacking of Instinct

I was fifteen when I realized that truth could be stolen, not with lies, but with power.

The adults around me didn't need to convince me that I'd done something wrong; they only needed to make me doubt my own body. That's how moral control begins, not through belief, but through humiliation.

The Day My Body Stopped Belonging to Me

It started when my diary went missing. It wasn't just paper; it was the only place I could be real. Inside were the things I wasn't allowed to say - desire, confusion, curiosity, love. When it vanished, I didn't just lose words; I lost ownership of my story.

What came after - the confrontation, the forced examination, the exile, was not just punishment, it was conditioning. It taught me that the body's voice was dangerous and must be silenced.

They called it protection.

It was programming.

When a child's truth is met with control instead of care, her nervous system learns that survival depends on compliance. Her heart beats fast, her throat closes, her thoughts scatter; that's biology's way of saying this isn't safe.

But in families built on fear, biology gets overridden by obligation.

The body says no.

Culture says you're ungrateful.

Religion says you're sinful.

And you learn to stay quiet, even when silence feels like dying.

How Obedience Rewrites the Brain

I didn't know it then, but what happened in those years was more than trauma; it was a full rewrite of my moral operating system. The body's instinct to seek safety, affection, and belonging was turned against me.

Each time I obeyed against my better judgment, the neural pathways of fear grew stronger. Each time I swallowed my truth, I reinforced the belief that speaking it would cost me everything.

That's how neuro-ethical hijacking works; your sense of right and wrong stops being self-generated and starts being externally sourced. You no longer ask, "Does this feel right in my body?" but "Will this keep me safe from punishment?"

It's not morality anymore - it's conditioning, and this is where neuro-ethical realism begins to matter - it recognizes that morality is not abstract. It's biological. The brain and the body record ethics as sensory information.

When you're raised in coercion, those moral circuits are literally rewired to avoid pain instead of pursuing truth.

The Biology of Fear-Based Morality

When you live in constant fear, your prefrontal cortex - the part of your brain that reasons and makes ethical decisions - goes offline. The amygdala, the fear centre, takes charge.

You stop processing options; you react.

You can't discern moral nuance when your body believes it's under attack.

This is why people under authoritarian systems, whether family, culture, or religion, often defend their abusers or traditions. It's not stupidity; it's neurological survival. Fear doesn't just silence the voice, it distorts the compass, and when fear becomes the moral teacher, guilt becomes the language of control.

I learned to apologize for breathing too loud. To hide joy because joy drew attention. To over-explain every action before anyone accused me of anything. That's what happens when a conscience is trained through shame. It no longer measures right and wrong; it measures danger.

The Cultural Machinery of Control

What my family called honour, the world often calls reputation. But both serve the same purpose: to protect appearances, even if it means destroying authenticity.

They believed they were saving me from shame, but what they really did was destroy trust - the core nutrient of conscience.

Without trust, ethics collapse into obedience.

That's why authoritarian cultures breed secrecy. When you can't safely tell the truth, you start performing a version of goodness that others will approve of. The more convincing the performance, the more disconnected the person.

And yet, that's the tragedy - society rewards the well-behaved, not the well-integrated.

From Survival to Awakening

There was a moment - after the move, after the surveillance, after the bars went up on my window, when I realized that if I stayed obedient, I would disappear completely. The instinct that had been beaten, shamed, and silenced began to whisper again.

It wasn't loud, but it was persistent: leave.

Leaving wasn't rebellion. It was biology reclaiming itself. It was the nervous system saying, enough.

This is what neuro-ethical realism is about: the moment instinct rises from beneath programming and chooses coherence over fear.

It's the body saying, this is wrong for me, even when every rule insists otherwise.

When I finally stepped out of that door, I wasn't chasing freedom; I was following the faint signal of conscience that still survived inside me. That was the most moral act I've ever committed.

The Anatomy of a Hijacked Instinct

If I break it down now - decades later -I can see the process clearly:

> 1. Violation of Trust: When the diary was taken, the first rupture occurred. The inner and outer world split.

> 2. Bodily Betrayal: The forced examination severed the link between body and safety.

> 3. Cultural Reinforcement: The relocation and shame narrative taught me that community acceptance mattered more than truth.

> 4. Fear Conditioning: Every punishment encoded a biological association between obedience and survival.

> 5. Disassociation: The psyche learned to leave the body to avoid pain; the final hijack.

And yet, inside all that, the instinct never died. It was just buried under hypervigilance.

When trauma survivors say they "don't trust themselves," what they really mean is that their nervous system learned to mislabel threat and safety. The work of neuro-ethical realism is the re-education of that system; teaching the body that truth no longer equals danger.

The Myth of Moral Purity

Looking back, I see how cultural and religious narratives use purity as a leash.

A woman's worth is tied to her body, not her being.

A man's worth is tied to dominance, not integrity.

And both are trained to distrust their own instincts because instinct threatens the hierarchy.

But purity isn't moral; it's mechanical. It keeps systems clean, not people whole.

The body, when allowed to feel, is not impure. It's honest, and honesty, in any repressive structure, is the real sin.

Learning to Listen Again

It took me years to relearn the language of my own biology; to know the difference between fear that warns and fear that lies.

That's where neuro-ethical healing begins: in discerning which signals are inherited, and which are authentic.

I began to ask different questions:

Does my chest tighten when I say yes?

Does my breath slow when I say no?

Does this action restore my dignity or reduce it?

That's the biological metric for morality. When the body relaxes, you're in truth. When it tenses, you're in conflict.

And that's not spirituality; that's neuroscience.

Reclaiming the Signal

My story is one of many, but it's also a map. Every survivor of moral conditioning carries the same quest: to return to the natural rhythm of conscience that existed before fear.

When you start making decisions that your body can rest inside, you become immune to manipulation. You don't need anyone's permission to be good; your biology already knows how.

Interlude: The Myth of Normal - Epigenetics and the Moral Genome

For generations, we were told that human nature was fixed, that goodness, madness, strength, and sin were inherited like hair colour.

It was a convenient myth. It allowed families, religions, and governments to declare who was born "better," who was "broken," and who should quietly disappear

But normal was never real.

Normal is a word that served those who benefited from sameness.

The rest of us - the traumatized, the outliers, the ones who felt too deeply - became the proof that humanity is in progress, not perfected.

Trauma as an Editor of the Genome

Biology used to be seen as a locked vault: you were born with your genes, and that was that. Now we know that experience itself - stress, love, danger, nurture - can turn those genes on and off like dimmer switches.

This is epigenetics: the body keeping score not in metaphor, but in methylation.

A mother's fear changes her child's cortisol receptors.

A soldier's startle reflex can echo in his son's heartbeat.

Generational trauma isn't folklore; it's physiology. When I say trauma changes DNA, I don't mean we become mutants. I mean that survival edits the script. We pass on new notes in the margin - warnings, sensitivities, instincts.

Every child is not a replica of their parents but a revision of reality - a body writing the next draft of adaptation.

Evolution never stopped; it just moved inside us.

Social Learning: The Second Genome

Then society enters, scalpel in hand. We tell children what to believe, who to fear, when to speak. We code their language with our doctrines and call it education.

That's how culture becomes the second genome - the one made not of molecules, but of messages.

But here's the limit of social control: you can teach, threaten, and shame all you like; if that child's biology senses incoherence, they will resist it. Some break the cycle not because they were taught how, but because their body refused to continue it.

Defiance isn't always rebellion.

Sometimes it's the body saying, "This isn't truth."

The Collapse of Eugenic Thinking

Once you understand that experience can alter the very expression of genes, the entire fantasy of "better breeding" falls apart.

Eugenics assumes purity; epigenetics proves plasticity.

You can't engineer morality into a population when morality itself is a dialogue between biology and experience. We are not manufacturing lines; we are moral ecosystems - dynamic, relational, responsive.

Evolution doesn't reward the pure, it rewards coherence.

Those who adapt, empathize, and self-correct - not those who conform - are the true continuation of humanity.

The Living Proof

Every survivor of trauma who becomes gentle instead of cruel,

every child who refuses to mirror the parent's abuse,

every person who learns to feel again after being numbed -

they are evolution in real time.

They are proof that DNA alone does not define destiny.

That normal was never the goal.

That our biology's highest function is not replication, it's repair.

Closing Reflection

Maybe this is what conscience really is: the body's long memory correcting the moral errors of its ancestors.

We are not born to perfect bloodlines.

We are born to perfect empathy.

And that - not control, not purity, not design - is the next stage of human evolution.

Closing Bridge

Chapter 2 of *Trial by Trust* was titled Time to Leave.

In Neuro-Ethical Realism, it becomes Time to Reclaim.

Leaving was not an act of defiance; it was the nervous system completing its moral cycle, saying *no,* where silence once meant survival.

This is where the philosophy begins to take shape: that conscience is not a rulebook handed down by authority, but an inner resonance sustained by the body itself, and once that resonance returns, there is no system, no culture, no past powerful enough to hijack it again.

That's the revolution of neuro-ethical realism: the return of instinct as moral authority.

CHAPTER 3

Reclaiming the Inner Compass

There's a point after breaking free when survival starts to feel like freedom, but it isn't yet.

It's just the absence of punishment.

I thought I had escaped control when I left home. But freedom without understanding your own programming is just relocation, not liberation.

The Mirage of Safety

When I drove away that night, my body believed I was running toward peace. The air smelled different, lighter, as though I'd finally broken the invisible leash that had held me since childhood. But the biology of fear doesn't dissolve just because you change your postcode; it follows you, coded into muscle memory.

The man I ran toward gave me what looked like safety - space to breathe, to be held, to belong somewhere. But when you've been trained to confuse protection with control, even love can feel like captivity in disguise.

That's how trauma works: it keeps showing you versions of itself until you learn the lesson. I didn't yet know what that lesson was. I just knew that the new life

I was stepping into wasn't the end of the story - it was a continuation of the experiment that had started in my childhood: what happens to conscience when it's rebuilt inside chaos.

The Body as Compass, Again

The first week after leaving, I barely slept. My body stayed on alert, even while my mind said, *you're safe now.*

That's the problem with trauma - the body doesn't listen to logic.

Every knock at the door felt like a test of loyalty. Every phone call was a possible threat. My nervous system was still calibrated to danger, waiting for the punishment that usually followed any act of self-choice. And yet, amid the noise, my inner compass started to twitch back to life.

When my sister attacked me in public - her hands around my throat, her eyes filled with rage - something strange happened: I didn't fight back. I didn't even hate her. I just held up my hands. That wasn't weakness. It was a decision. A primitive line drawn by conscience saying: I will not replicate what broke me.

That's the moment I began to understand; morality is not about who wins the fight, it's about who refuses to become the thing they escaped.

The Science of False Calm

Psychologists call it fawning: the reflex to appease your aggressor to stay alive.

I call it learned diplomacy - survival dressed as grace.

That night, as my family's anger hunted us through supermarkets and driveways, I thought calmness meant maturity. It didn't. It meant my brain had switched into preservation mode, releasing chemicals that made me still, quiet, compliant.

To outsiders, that looked like composure. Inside, it was paralysis.

That's how the hijack continues; you appear functional, but your ethics are still being run on fear's software.

Neuro-ethical realism views this not as character flaw but as neurobiology in self-defense: the body creates moral stillness when moral chaos overwhelms it.

Love and the Illusion of Agency

People often ask why survivors "choose" unhealthy relationships. They don't see that choice only exists when the brain feels safe enough to imagine options.

At sixteen, when I agreed to marriage, it wasn't romance or rebellion. It was refuge. A child raised in surveillance doesn't crave passion; she craves absence of threat, and yet, inside that fragile arrangement, there was sincerity. He treated me with care, bought me things I'd never owned, said he'd protect me. For the first time, someone looked at me as worthy of choosing. My body mistook that for love, because affection had always been conditional.

What I didn't realize was that my conscience was still outsourced; I was still seeking validation instead of alignment.

That's the residue of moral trauma: the need for someone else to approve your freedom before you believe it's real.

The Physics of Consequence

Then came the call. My sister's voice - cold, trembling:

"Dads gone. He took his own life. Don't come to the funeral."

Grief doesn't just shatter you; it resets your entire neuro-ethical field[1]. In that moment, every justification,

---

[1] When I refer to the neuro-ethical Field, I mean the living interface between biology and morality, the space where neural, emotional, and physiological processes converge to produce conscience. It is both metaphor and observation: a way of describing how coherence within the body gives rise to moral awareness. This concept is grounded in neurobiology, not metaphysics; it reflects my book's central premise that morality emerges from biological alignment rather than social construction.

every attempt to be brave, collapsed. My body went weightless. Then numb.

Here's what neuro-ethical realism teaches about such moments: when the mind can't integrate an event, the body becomes the archive. The muscles remember the screams, the sweat, the collapse - even when words won't form.

I blamed myself, because guilt is the body's attempt to make chaos logical. If it's my fault, then maybe the world still makes sense.

But guilt is not the same as responsibility, and yet, for years, I lived as if it was - returning to his grave, apologizing, offering flowers as moral restitution. I didn't understand then that this ritual wasn't about him; it was about reconciling with my own conscience, the one that had been forced to grow inside contradiction.

The Cycle of Reconstruction

The following years were like rebuilding a house without blueprints; I finished school, learned new skills, found temporary peace in small routines - making tea, studying, watching light move across the windowpane.

Each act of normality was therapy for a nervous system that had never known consistency. But underneath, the architecture of fear still trembled.

The neighbours, the whispers, the judgment; they became the new overseers. Instead of parents, there were gossipers. Instead of priests, there were moral spectators. The stage changed; the script stayed the same: be acceptable or be outcast.

It took me a long time to see that society simply rebrands control in prettier language.

In families, it's called honour.

In communities, reputation.

In workplaces, professionalism.

All are versions of the same hierarchy: obedience over authenticity.

Neural Repair Begins

Healing didn't start with forgiveness. It started with education; with the simple act of naming what was happening inside me. Every time I learned a new concept - trauma response, fawn reflex, neural rewiring - my brain lit up. Not metaphorically, literally. Understanding created neurochemical relief.

It meant I wasn't crazy; I was conditioned.

That's why knowledge feels sacred to the wounded; it gives language to what pain made wordless, and that language rewires the moral brain.

Neuro-ethical realism recognizes that intellectual awareness is not separate from healing, it is healing.

When the brain can finally name its oppressor, the conscience reclaims its coordinates.

The Moral Mathematics of Survival

Years later, when I reconciled with my mother, I saw the equation of human ethics in its rawest form:

She was both the victim and the enforcer.

She loved me and blamed me.

She apologized and repeated the same control patterns.

In ordinary logic, that's hypocrisy. In neuro-ethical logic, it's looped programming: trauma so deeply inherited it becomes culture.

Understanding that didn't excuse the harm, but it ended the confusion. I stopped expecting coherence from incoherence. I stopped trying to win moral approval from people still running survival code, and that's when peace became possible, not from being forgiven, but from no longer needing to be.

Motherhood as Biological Redemption

When I became pregnant, fear returned in a new disguise - this time, the terror of repeating the cycle.

Would I pass on my disconnection? Would my daughter inherit my silence?

That's when my body, again, became teacher. It softened instead of hardening. It demanded nourishment, rest, and slowness.

Motherhood forced me to slow the tempo of my nervous system, to relearn the pace of safety. Each heartbeat of my child was an ethical metronome, reminding me that protection without control is possible.

That's the biological proof of recovery: when instinct finally learns that love and fear are not the same thing.

The Return of Self-Authority

By the time my mother re-entered my life, I was no longer seeking approval, only understanding.

I accepted her contradictions because I finally understood my own. We are all products of what our nervous systems could tolerate.

Some of us freeze.

Some fight.

Some fawn.

Some flee.

But the rare few, the ones who turn survival into wisdom, begin to watch the reactions and rewrite them.

That's the work of conscience.

Not moral perfection, but moral authorship.

The Philosophy in Summary

Neuro-ethical realism argues that conscience is not divine, nor cultural, it's neurological feedback refined by lived experience.

When trauma distorts that feedback, life becomes a laboratory for recalibration. Each mistake, each reconciliation, each heartbreak - these aren't moral failures; they're ethical data points.

Through reflection and biology, conscience re-stabilizes.

My story shows the formula:

1. Pain reveals pattern.

2. Pattern reveals programming.

3. Awareness reclaims agency.

4. Agency restores integrity.

That's how the inner compass is rebuilt, not through confession or compliance, but through coherence.

Closing Reflection

I once thought morality was about doing right by others. Now I know it's about doing right with yourself first, because until your body feels safe in your own truth, every good deed is just a performance to avoid punishment.

But when safety and honesty coexist, that's when conscience stops whispering and starts leading.

That's when freedom finally feels real.

CHAPTER 4

The Architecture of Consequence

Motherhood didn't start with bliss. It started with pain so deep that it made me question the very nature of creation.

The first scream in the delivery room wasn't just physical, it was existential. It was my body learning that nature's idea of life doesn't always align with our idea of mercy.

The First Lesson in Biological Truth

When my daughter tore her way into the world, I felt every law of biology collapse into one command: survive this moment.

No theology, no social doctrine, just the body's raw intelligence doing what it was designed to do.

That's when I realized something essential about ethics: morality begins in pain.

Not as punishment, but as awareness.

The moment you endure suffering you didn't choose, your conscience records the data. It learns compassion from exposure, not instruction. Pain isn't divine retribution; it's biological instruction.

Neuro-ethical realism calls this the initiation of consequence; the point where biology teaches you what abstract morality never could: that every choice carries cost in flesh.

How the Body Stores Moral Memory

Childbirth leaves a scar that doesn't fade, even when it heals. For weeks I couldn't walk. I'd sit, dizzy, trying to breastfeed, my chest cracked and burning, my body trembling from exhaustion. Everyone told me, "It's normal."

That word, *normal*, became the soft glove over cruelty.

When no milk came, they told me to keep trying, that it was my duty as a woman. My body begged me to stop; my conscience whispered that my child was starving.

Culture said endure.

Biology said adapt.

When I finally gave her the bottle and she slept peacefully for the first time, I learned one of the most sacred truths of neuro-ethical realism: compassion is when conscience overrides expectation.

That act - disobeying tradition to protect my child - was moral evolution in real time. The body had been screaming the truth for a long time before anyone gave me permission to listen.

The Invisible Architecture of Control

After Mum left and the house fell silent, I began to see the invisible architecture of consequence everywhere. Every tradition, every "should," every unspoken rule of womanhood was designed to keep me compliant; to make me mistake endurance for virtue.

They said I should be grateful. That my husband worked hard. That I was lucky to be provided for.

But what they meant was: don't want more.

I was twenty, intelligent, ambitious, capable; and completely contained.

The cage just looked different now: no longer bars and threats, but social smiles and phrases like "you have everything a woman could want." That's how systemic morality hides in plain sight; by turning the very language of gratitude into a leash.

The Science of Diminishment

When a person is told repeatedly that their role is enough, the brain's reward circuitry begins to adapt.

Desire shrinks to fit survival.

Dreams down-regulate.

And soon, the body forgets what expansion even feels like.

I thought my restlessness was depression. But looking back, I see it was conscience refusing to accept smallness.

Neuro-ethical realism calls this moral inflammation: the biological irritation that occurs when your lived reality contradicts your innate capacity.

It's not sin. It's the body rejecting ethical stagnation.

Consequences as Teachers

My daughter's hunger taught me to trust my instincts.

My body's pain taught me to listen deeper.

My mother's absence taught me resilience.

And later, my son's birth - with all its terror and blood and miraculous survival - taught me the anatomy of consequence itself: that sometimes life tests your moral structure to see if it can hold under collapse.

Every contraction was both physical and symbolic; the body building and breaking ethical structure at once.

To birth is to cooperate with consequence.

To mother is to live inside it daily.

The Economics of Sacrifice

They said I was being looked after - that I didn't need to work, that I was lucky.

But what they meant was: be dependent, stay quiet.

Every dollar I didn't earn became a vote against my autonomy. Every time I was told we couldn't afford something, I felt another wall rise between who I was and who I was allowed to be.

Dependence breeds ethical distortion.

When survival depends on someone else's approval, the truth becomes a luxury you can't afford. And so, obedience masquerades as partnership.

That's how moral erosion begins - not in abuse, but in subtle financial control that makes integrity too expensive to maintain.

The Dissolution of Idealism

When I looked at my husband - the man I once believed was my rescuer - I began to see the reflection of my father: the same dismissiveness, the same moral hierarchy, the same gentle belittling that eats at a person's sense of self.

I started to understand that love without equality becomes captivity dressed as care. It promises safety but costs individuality, and soon, your moral compass points only toward keeping peace.

But peace kept at the expense of truth isn't peace, it's sedation.

When Compassion Turns to Clarity

By the time my second child was born, something in me had shifted.

I still loved, but I stopped worshipping.

I still cared, but I stopped obeying.

That's when conscience grew teeth.

I began to question:

Why is my ambition seen as greed?

Why is my exhaustion invisible?

Why is my silence still expected to be gratitude?

These weren't rebellious questions; they were neurological awakenings.

Because once you start living in alignment with your biology again, lies lose their authority.

The Architecture Itself

Every human life, when viewed through neuro-ethical realism, is built upon a tri-structure:

1. Instinct (the biological base) - the body's immediate response to truth or threat.

2. Conditioning (the cultural overlay) - the learned responses shaped by family, faith, and fear.

3. Consequence (the integrative system) - the outcome of what happens when the first two collide.

When instinct and conditioning align, life feels coherent. When they clash, consequences emerge - sometimes as pain, sometimes as awareness.

I lived most of my early years trapped between the two - body truth versus cultural obedience. But consequence became my teacher, not my punishment.

That's what this chapter of life proved: you can't escape consequence, but you can refine it.

You can't avoid pain, but you can extract meaning.

That's the only ethical architecture that holds.

The Deconstruction of False Hierarchies

When my mother-in-law came to stay, I realized how hierarchy weaves itself into domestic life like a virus.

Gold bangles, deference, "proper" daughter-in-law behaviour; all signals of worth in a system designed to measure women against each other.

It's not just cultural; it's neurological.

Comparison triggers the same survival circuits as physical threat. That's why so many women end up policing one another; it's biology hijacked by patriarchy.

But I couldn't keep performing. I didn't care about the jewellery, the gossip, the silent ranking system. I was done playing games that made everyone smaller.

That defiance wasn't pride, it was coherence.

When Consequence Becomes Clarity

When I lost my dog, when I failed to find joy, when I drove an old car through life that barely held together, those weren't just hardships. They were reflections of my internal architecture collapsing so that a new one could form.

Each external loss mirrored an internal correction. I started to see cause and effect not as cosmic justice but as feedback loops: life continually mirroring your state until you evolve.

That's the heart of neuro-ethical realism: the understanding that consequence isn't punishment, it's calibration.

Every event, no matter how cruel, adjusts you closer to your authentic coordinates.

Emergence of the New Self

By the time I began studying again, working toward accounting and a future I could claim, the architecture had started to rebuild - brick by brick, choice by choice, consequence by consequence.

I was still young, just twenty, but my inner structure was older than most people's entire belief systems.

I had lived the science of conscience.

I had felt the physics of consequence in every cell.

And I knew this:

I didn't leave home to end up destroyed again.

If life was going to test me, then I'd use every test to design something indestructible - integrity that didn't need permission.

Closing Reflection - The Physics of Moral Gravity

Everything we do falls somewhere in the gravitational field of consequence. You can try to escape it - through denial, religion, control - but the field always wins. The only freedom is to understand its geometry and move within it consciously.

That's what I was learning then, between babies, between disappointments, between breaths: that my body had been the architect all along.

Every pain, every rebellion, every moment of clarity; they were blueprints, and finally, I was ready to start building.

CHAPTER 5

The Echo of Pattern

Freedom never announces itself politely. It creeps in first as disobedience.

At twenty-four, I was done being the polite version of myself - the one who kept saying yes to men who fed on my guilt, to cultures that mistook control for care, and to a God filtered through male translation.

I wasn't chasing chaos; I was chasing agency, and that pursuit - messy, hormonal, bruised, and human - became my next moral classroom.

Desire as Data

Every time I sought love outside my marriage, people said I was "falling." But falling implies losing control. What I was doing was testing gravity, seeing how deep conscience runs when every rule around you is rigged.

When you're starved for validation, even crumbs feel like a feast.

Neuro-ethical realism calls this the emotional scarcity loop: where unmet biological needs for belonging and safety override conditioned notions of right and wrong.

The body doesn't care about dogma; it cares about regulation. It seeks equilibrium through connection, even forbidden connection. So, when affection arrived disguised as danger, I didn't rationalize it; I responded to it.

That's what trauma does, it rewires your moral GPS around survival, not virtue.

The Body's Rebellion Against Ownership

He had claimed my labour, my image, my time, even my guilt. The only thing left that still felt mine was my desire, and that, too, I was taught to repress.

So, when I finally felt desired, not as property but as presence, my nervous system lit up like it was rediscovering oxygen.

That kiss wasn't sin; it was feedback.

It told me: you are still alive.

Desire, in this context, wasn't about lust. It was the body's ethical protest against de-humanization. When systems deny you agency, even misdirected rebellion is a step toward coherence.

Violence as Cultural Reflex

The night the window shattered was the night culture showed its true face; control always breaks glass before it breaks people.

He didn't need to scream religion or masculinity; the ritual was already encoded. The breaking, the silence, the unspoken threat, all of it was the choreography of inherited power.

That's the cruel irony: patriarchy doesn't need belief; it just needs repetition.

He hit me because he could - because he had been taught that consequence is his to administer, and repentance is mine to perform.

That's not love, that's moral outsourcing.

Aftermath: The Collapse of False Morality

When the bruises turned yellow and the guilt calcified, I learned something crucial: shame is a social tool, not a divine one. It's how systems make individuals self-police. I was ashamed not because I was immoral, but because I'd been trained to feel immoral for wanting freedom.

That's when I stopped apologizing to God and started demanding explanations from the world. Religion said

I'd invited demons; neuroscience said my nervous system was overloaded.

Guess which one helped me heal?

The Anatomy of Awakening

The more I studied fitness, the more I began to see the correlation between muscle and morality.

When you strengthen your body, you start noticing the tension between what you're told to endure and what your body actually endures. Strength training became symbolic - it was resistance in literal form.

Each rep whispered, you are reclaiming territory.

Each drop of sweat rewired a belief.

I wasn't sculpting abs; I was sculpting conscience.

Neuro-ethical realism frames this as somatic sovereignty: the reclaiming of bodily autonomy as the first stage of moral autonomy.

The Mirror of Desire

Meeting her - the woman who would unravel everything I thought I knew about attraction - was like holding up a mirror that reflected only honesty.

She wasn't "temptation"; she was evidence, evidence that goodness doesn't conform to doctrine, that empathy, humour, and authenticity are more divine than any sermon.

I had been told gay people were cursed, yet she showed more compassion than most men of faith I'd ever known.

So, who was really lost?

That question detonated years of conditioning. Because when experience contradicts indoctrination, integrity demands that you trust experience.

Morality without reality is just theatre.

The Neurology of Truth

When I examined the surge of warmth I felt around her, I realized it wasn't "sin." It was serotonin. When I cried at her kindness, it wasn't weakness; it was the ventral vagus nerve reactivating after years of suppression.

The body doesn't lie; it just communicates in chemistry.

That's the biological basis of neuro-ethical realism: truth is what regulates you; lies are what dysregulate you.

By that measure, the pews of devotion had been making me sick long before desire ever did.

Moral Dissonance and the Question of God

If God created biology, then condemning biology is blasphemy.

To tell someone their orientation is an error is to accuse the Creator of malpractice. The older I got, the more I saw how religion wasn't protecting morality; it was protecting hierarchy.

It wasn't about God; it was about control, and once I saw that, I couldn't unsee it.

So, when I kissed her - the woman I was taught to fear - I wasn't betraying God.

I was betraying a lie.

The Science of Unlearning

Every time I questioned a rule, my anxiety spiked; that was the old circuitry firing, warning me that defiance equals danger.

But each time I survived the guilt, the neural pathway weakened.

That's what growth looks like neurologically: repetition of truth until the lie loses charge.

Forgiveness, I learned, is not about excusing others, it's about re-coding your own nervous system to stop expecting justice from abusers.

Violence, Fear, and the Parasite of Guilt

When he stood over me again, threatening, accusing, weaponizing forgiveness, I realized something chilling: his calm was the quiet of a man who believed consequence didn't apply to him.

He thought his violence was justified because my rebellion embarrassed him.

That's what cultural programming does; it fuses ego with righteousness.

But every time I refused to internalize his hatred, I starved the parasite of guilt a little more. Freedom isn't a switch; it's a starvation process.

When Love Returns Dressed as Repentance

When he begged me to come home, voice soft, eyes fake-sorry, I almost believed him.

Not because he changed, but because I still wanted to believe someone could. The trauma bond is chemical. It tricks you into mistaking familiarity for safety.

Oxytocin, dopamine, cortisol - all playing their sick duet.

Returning home wasn't weakness; it was neurology, and that's what so many people don't understand about "why she stayed."

It's not stupidity, it's circuitry.

Moral Equilibrium: The End of Obedience

When I finally took off the veil, I wasn't rejecting modesty, I was rejecting hypocrisy. It wasn't rebellion against faith; it was allegiance to truth. My body had been suffocating under inherited symbolism. Removing it was my nervous system exhaling after years of moral asthma.

I didn't stop believing in goodness, I just stopped outsourcing it.

The Lesson Beneath the Chaos

Everything that happened - the affair, the violence, the lesbian awakening, the abortion, the guilt - it all had one recurring pattern: the collision between biology and belief.

Every collapse was data.

Every heartbreak was a calibration.

Every mistake was a measurement of coherence.

That's what consequence really is - feedback from reality reminding you what's sustainable for your integrity.

Closing Reflection - The Echo of Pattern

The echo of pattern is what we mistake for fate. We keep repeating what we haven't resolved. But once awareness enters the loop, repetition becomes reflection.

By twenty-five, I wasn't yet free, but I was awake, and awakening, I've learned, is the only kind of redemption that's real.

CHAPTER 6

Cognitive Dissonance and the Cost of Clarity

Truth rarely enters like a whisper. Sometimes, it crashes through the window holding a cleaver. That was the night I stopped pretending peace was holy. Fear had been my religion far longer than faith ever was.

The Fire That Burned the Pretence

The bushfire season mirrored my internal one. Whole regions burning, skies red as punishment, and I stood there, towel in hand, trying to sunbake, as if life were normal.

That's what denial looks like in practice: trying to tan while the world combusts.

Black Saturday wasn't just a tragedy outside; it was a reflection of my own combustion. Every woman who's lived in silent tension knows that heat - the pressure of unspoken resentment, the smoke of words unsaid.

Nature had become my mirror; she burned where I refused to speak.

When Comfort Is Just a Controlled Burn

Our holidays, our new houses, the endless relocations, they looked like progress, but they were avoidance dressed as stability. Each move promised renewal but delivered repetition. Every unpacked box carried the same ghosts.

Five houses in eleven years; that wasn't adventure; it was displacement therapy. When you don't feel safe in your own skin, you keep changing walls.

The fig tree in the backyard was the only thing that made sense. It gave without permission, without guilt, without condition. It reminded me that abundance was possible, but only in ecosystems that allow growth, not choke it.

Cognitive Dissonance: The Split Between Truth and Tolerance

I used to think strength meant staying calm while being disrespected. Now I know that was just moral anesthesia; a trick of the nervous system to stop you from noticing your own erasure.

He'd scream, punch walls, and then offer explanations that twisted logic into obligation. I nodded, because I'd been trained that nodding keeps you alive.

That's what cognitive dissonance feels like; the nervous system bowing while the conscience screams get out.

Neuro-ethical realism names this ethical overload: when your biological instinct and your social conditioning pull in opposite directions until conscience fractures.

The Inheritance of Violence

When the soap-dish shard cut my son's back, time froze. I saw my father's fists replay through another man's hands. I had become the bridge connecting two generations of trauma.

That's the cruel mathematics of unconsciousness, pain unexamined becomes policy. Families pass it down not as legacy, but as reflex. I had sworn I would never repeat what I'd lived through, yet here it was, dressed differently but speaking the same language.

That night I understood that violence doesn't begin with the first strike, it begins the moment silence becomes strategy.

The Search for Function in a System Built to Break You

When I applied to join the police, I wasn't chasing authority, I was testing whether justice could exist inside a system that had failed me. Getting pulled over for speeding on my way to the recruitment session felt almost prophetic; the law reminding me who it really serves.

I wanted to enforce fairness, but fairness doesn't thrive in structures built on obedience.

So, I found another way: dentistry.

At first glance, it was small, almost trivial - fixing teeth while my own life decayed. But there, in that sterile light, I rediscovered autonomy.

Patients came and went, and I helped them heal. No violence, no control, just steady hands and clean tools.

That's what freedom looks like when you've lived through tyranny: the simple ability to work without fear.

The Neurochemistry of Independence

Each paycheck released a dose of dopamine my marriage had long suppressed. Money wasn't greed, it was permission. Earning meant I could breathe without asking for air.

That's the neuro-ethical truth of financial independence: the prefrontal cortex finally gets to plan without the amygdala screaming danger.

Freedom, it turns out, is a chemical event as much as a moral one.

Parenting Under Pressure: The Mirror and the Mask

My daughter's silence became the mirror I couldn't look away from. Her darkness, her bandaged arm, that was my reflection filtered through adolescence. She was internalizing what I'd modelled: survival through suppression.

When I found the scars, I wanted to scream, not at her but at the system that breeds despair and calls it discipline. Yet even then, I reached for the same old script - moral panic, religious fear, control disguised as care. I became what I hated, because culture is a parasite; it lives through the hosts who think they've escaped it.

That's when I learned the hardest truth of neuro-ethical realism: healing doesn't start when you stop hurting others; it starts when you stop passing on the programming.

Retaliation as Primitive Justice

When I stormed the school grounds with backup, it wasn't rational, it was ancestral. That wasn't revenge; it was my nervous system re-enacting protection it had never received. We were three women walking in with the energy of ten generations who'd been told to stay quiet. Fear left our bodies that day, even if diplomacy did too.

Was it right? No.

Was it ethical in the biological sense? Absolutely, my body restored equilibrium by proving to itself that defense was possible.

That's how suppressed systems reboot: through confrontation before comprehension.

Spiritual Contact and Neurological Release

When the rush came - the tremor, the goosebumps, the sudden surge of peace - I thought it was divine.

Maybe it was.

But neuroscience would later tell me it was the body finally releasing years of cortisol in one electric discharge.

Some people call it enlightenment; I call it a full system reset.

That's when the cleaver incident happened. He accused, I sat still, and the world stopped. For once, fear didn't win. I'd been preparing for that confrontation my entire life; rehearsing courage in dreams, practicing detachment in pain.

When he swung that cleaver, the blade didn't just cut the watermelon, it sliced through my last illusion: that love could coexist with domination.

Digital Liberation

Facebook became my confessional, my classroom, my rebellion. While he feared technology, I used it to build invisible doors. In that space, I met voices from worlds he couldn't reach - men, women, thinkers, strangers.

Some were kind, some toxic, some catalysts. Each message was a neuron firing toward freedom.

That's how modern liberation begins - not in protests, but in private messages typed with trembling hands.

The Illusion of Connection

When I met the man online - the one who seemed gentle, scarred, empathetic, I didn't fall in love.

I fell into possibility.

He represented the version of masculinity I'd been told didn't exist: emotional, respectful, spiritual. Whether he was real or not didn't matter, the idea was.

In neuro-ethical terms, he was a symbolic corrective: the brain's way of proving safety is conceivable.

Sometimes healing first arrives as illusion; reality catches up later.

The Cost of Clarity

Clarity is expensive.

It costs delusion, comfort, belonging, sometimes reputation. When I started listening to my own conscience instead of others' expectations, I lost entire communities.

But I gained a coherent nervous system.

That's the bargain of awareness: peace in exchange for people.

The Rise of Cognitive Integrity

Neuro-ethical realism defines cognitive integrity as the alignment of three systems:

1. Truth perception: the capacity to notice contradiction without denying it.

2. Moral regulation: the body's physiological response to authenticity versus deceit.

3. Ethical action: behaviour consistent with internal coherence, not external pressure.

By that definition, I wasn't sinful or rebellious, I was recalibrating. I was becoming neurologically aligned with reality, and that's why everything had to burn - the marriage, the illusions, the false peace.

You can't rebuild conscience on corrupted code.

Closing Reflection - The Rise, The Fall, The Fire

Everything that fell apart was a purification, not a punishment.

Every house that burned, every fight that erupted, every scar that appeared - they were all indicators of system overload releasing itself. The fire outside mirrored the fire within, and from those ashes, a different morality began to take shape, one not borrowed, not inherited, but biologically authored.

I call it Cognitive Integrity: the moment your mind and body finally agree on the same version of truth.

CHAPTER 7

The Fracture and the Field

I thought freedom meant distance. Turns out, it meant confrontation, with every pattern I'd mistaken for love.

When I drove north toward Queensland, leaving Melbourne behind, the road hummed like a test of faith. Every kilometre felt like shedding old skin, every highway sign a nervous-system checkpoint asking: Do you still want this?

I told myself it was a road trip, but deep down, I knew it was an autopsy.

I was dissecting my own history in motion.

The Illusion of Escape

We convince ourselves that new scenery equals new self. But biology travels with you. Trauma doesn't care about postal codes.

In neuro-ethical realism, this is called the migration illusion: the belief that external change can pre-empt internal evolution.

But neurons don't obey geography. They obey memory.

I thought I was driving away from control; in truth, I was driving straight into another version of it. The universe had queued the next test: same theme, new face.

The Englishman

When he appeared, all polished accent and quiet wounds, I thought the story was changing. He wasn't like the others - softer, apologetic, attentive.

He called me "kind," and for a moment, I mistook attention for alignment.

That's how trauma seduces you; it disguises familiarity as destiny. The nervous system recognises the pattern before the mind does, but because pain once felt like love, we follow the echo instead of the instinct.

He told me he was gentle.

He told me he'd been hurt.

He told me everything that would justify me fixing him.

And because I was wired to earn love through service, I took the job.

The Fracture Point

The body always knows before the brain does.

The night I ignored the alarm bells - the small tremor of unease, the subtle tightening in my chest when he pulled out that joint- I effectively silenced my moral sensor.

Neuro-ethical realism calls this ethical override: when your conscience recognises threat but your conditioning insists on compassion.

It's how good people walk themselves into bad situations, not through stupidity, but through programming.

That night, I chose tolerance over truth, and the fracture widened.

When Attraction Masks Repetition

The chemistry was undeniable - electric, disarming, intoxicating. But attraction is not evidence of compatibility; it's evidence of exposure. You're drawn to what mirrors your earliest unresolved experience.

His neediness matched my instinct to rescue.

His insecurity activated my caretaker circuitry.

We fit perfectly, like two broken bones trying to heal each other but instead rubbing raw.

That's what happens when two traumas fall in love; the relationship becomes a laboratory for pattern replication, and the lesson only begins when one of you stops repeating.

The Neuro-Ethics of Desire

Desire isn't immoral; it's informational.

It tells you where your energy still seeks coherence. But when desire is driven by absence rather than authenticity, it becomes a feedback loop of depletion.

He wasn't my soulmate; he was my syllabus.

The curriculum was simple:

1. Recognise repetition.

2. End the pattern.

3. Integrate the lesson without needing the pain.

But I wasn't there yet. I was still addicted to narrative; the idea that love redeems chaos.

Jealousy as a Nervous Reflex

When he accused me of flirting with strangers on balconies, I saw the ghost of every insecure man before him. The tone was different, but the vibration was identical - fear disguised as possession. That's when I understood: jealousy isn't passion; it's the nervous system's allergic reaction to uncertainty.

In neuro-ethical realism, jealousy is classed as empathic inversion: an emotion that misinterprets connection as competition.

It's not evil; it's unrefined empathy. But in immature hands, it becomes a weapon.

The Mirror of Guilt

He called me manipulative, then apologized and said he loved me.

That's how abusers secure control; not through continuous cruelty, but through intermittent kindness. The inconsistency is what keeps you hooked; the brain releases dopamine in anticipation of reward, not reward itself, and so, you stay.

You rationalize. You empathize.

You tell yourself he's damaged, and you'll help him heal.

But that's not love - that's moral labour.

Addiction to Apology

He'd lash out, then cry, then tell me I was the only person who understood him.

That's the classic trauma loop: abuse, guilt, affection, repeat - each apology rewires your conscience to tolerate the next wound.

Forgiveness becomes pathology - it's not about mercy; it's about avoiding dissonance.

You'd rather believe in the potential of goodness than accept the permanence of harm.

That's what I was paying for, not love, but coherence.

The Return of the Patriarch

When I finally drove home, sunburnt, exhausted, halfway between relief and regret, I walked into a familiar hell: the husband who used "forgiveness" as a form of surveillance.

He dragged me to the garage, weight plate in hand, screaming, trembling, demanding confession, and yet, even then, the words that left my mouth weren't mine; the prayers were a reflex taught for dying well, not for living honestly. My body was praying for coherence; my upbringing was praying for heaven.

That moment taught me the deepest lesson of neuro-ethical realism: we are not born liars, but we are taught whose truths to speak.

Violence as Moral Feedback

When he slammed the weight beside my head instead of through it, I felt no gratitude, only confirmation.

The experiment was complete; love built on fear collapses under truth.

Violence is never random; it's feedback from incoherence reaching critical mass. That moment wasn't punishment, it was data, and the data was clear: survival requires separation.

That's how consequence teaches - through collapse first, clarity later.

The False Redemption Cycle

When he cried and begged to return, I saw it all like a lab report:

The sympathetic system flaring (fear of loss).

The parasympathetic system hijacked (pseudo-remorse).

The reward circuit whispering promises it couldn't fund.

Forgiveness wouldn't change him because forgiveness can't rewire someone else's brain, it can only release yours.

And so, I stopped performing mercy.

I told him to leave.

The Fracture of Illusion

The Englishman lingered, hovering between obsession and worship. His infatuation fed my ego but drained my coherence. I mistook intensity for intimacy - again.

That's when I realized: I had become fluent in dysfunction, and fluency is dangerous when you forget it's a survival language.

When he blamed me for his own guilt, when he claimed I made him sin, when his love turned accusatory, that was the moment the fracture reached the core. The part of me that once needed to be chosen finally chose itself.

The Field Revealed

Neuro-ethical realism proposes that every human exists inside a moral field; a network of emotional, neurological, and energetic exchanges that regulate equilibrium.

When you violate your own truth, the field constricts.

When you act in coherence, it expands.

The people you attract are reflections of your field's frequency. When your boundaries blur, you draw mirrors, not matches.

The Englishman wasn't evil; he was informational; an algorithm of my unresolved self. Every interaction was the field teaching me: "Stop confusing intensity for alignment. Stop calling suffering destiny."

Integration

When I finally sat alone -no husband, no lover, no noise - I noticed something unfamiliar: silence that didn't feel like absence. It felt like calibration. My nervous system was finally operating on home frequency.

That's what healing is: Not happiness, not revenge, just coherence. The ability to exist without seeking correction.

I understood then that the field isn't external; it's biological. It's what conscience becomes once it stops being afraid.

Closing Reflection - The Fracture and the Field

Every pattern I broke became an opening.

Every person I lost became a neuron rewiring.

Every fracture revealed more light.

Love doesn't save you from consequence; it is consequence; when fully understood, it no longer hurts, it instructs. As I looked back on all the wreckage, I realized:

None of it was wasted. It was just the field, guiding me home.

CHAPTER 8

The Descent into Duality

Every collapse begins with a contradiction you're too tired to confront. This one started the moment I mistook obsession for devotion. He spoke with that soft English calm, the kind that makes chaos sound intelligent. My family adored him. They saw what I wanted them to see; a man who looked gentle, prayed on time, complimented my cooking, respected elders.

But beneath that charm was the same addiction to control that every patriarch carries; it just wore better cologne.

The Dual Face of Devotion

He was both the victim and the villain of his own story. One minute, he wept over curses and demons; the next, he blamed me for summoning them. He said love was sacred but lit joints like offerings to his anxiety.

Neuro-ethically, that's split-state behaviour: the brain toggling between guilt and gratification, never resting in coherence.

Religion had taught him repentance could erase repetition; that confession cancels consequences. But biology doesn't work that way. The nervous system remembers everything.

He called it "faith."

I called it dissociation.

Cognitive Dissonance Disguised as Care

He told me I was the only one who truly saw him. Then accused me of inviting spirits into the house. He spoke of God's tests while hiding weed under the bed.

That's the thing about hypocrisy, it's not always intentional. It's just the collision of an undeveloped conscience with a convenient belief system.

Every argument turned into theology.

Every apology turned into strategy.

Every silence became punishment.

And still, I stayed, because part of me was addicted to hope, the dopamine rush of potential change.

The Second Phone

Discovery isn't revelation; it's confrontation.

The night I unlocked his second phone, my hands trembled not from fear, but recognition. There it was, the proof that intuition had been screaming for months. His ex, the messages, the half-truths, the recycled lies.

But the shock wasn't about betrayal; it was about pattern.

I'd lived this déjà vu before: the hidden device, the secret world, the way men protected their lies like relics.

Neuro-ethical realism calls this loop conditioning: when repeated betrayal teaches your brain that vigilance equals safety.

You become your own detective because trust feels like negligence.

The Religious Trapdoor

When cornered, he didn't apologize, he spiritualized[2].

"The spirits are trying to turn you against me," he said.

That line deserves a chapter of its own in humanity's manual of manipulation.

He wasn't invoking faith; he was outsourcing responsibility.

---

[2] This section examines moral decision-making through the lens of biological coherence, not theology. It explores how the body recognises truth or contradiction within moral narratives, rather than debating doctrine.

That's how religion gets weaponized; it turns morality into an external authority so that accountability can be deferred.

But conscience, in its pure biological form, doesn't defer.

It records.

Every deception leaves residue in the body - tight jaw, shallow breath, racing pulse.

That's moral data, not metaphor.

When Belief Becomes a Hostage Situation

He said my skepticism was proof I'd been possessed. That's when I realized religion and gaslighting use the same syntax:

"You're lost unless you agree with me."

It wasn't just him; it was centuries of indoctrination speaking through him. He'd been programmed to believe authority equals love, and obedience equals virtue.

The rest of us just inherited the aftertaste.

The Pregnancy Paradox

When the test turned positive, time slowed. He smiled like a convert finally rewarded. I stared at the line as if it were a sentence.

He saw creation; I saw captivity. For him, it proved divine blessing. For me, it exposed biological betrayal; my body cooperating with a man my soul had already rejected.

That's the essence of duality: the body doing what it was designed to do while the conscience begs it to stop.

Free will becomes a spectator sport.

The Public Trial

He called my sister to report my "disobedience."

He turned pregnancy into prosecution.

Watching him plead his case to my family, speaking of "sin" and "God's plan," I understood how patriarchy survives - through performance.

He wasn't protecting life; he was protecting dominance.

He used moral language to mask control, quoting scripture like a legal clause. But underneath it all was terror; the fear of losing ownership over the one thing he thought he'd finally conquered: a woman who could think for herself.

The Collapse of Faith

I once believed religion guided conscience. Now I saw how often it replaces it.

If belief demands blindness, it's not belief, it's anesthesia.

My family meant well, but even they defaulted to doctrine before empathy. When they said, "It's God's will," what they meant was, "We're afraid to choose." Fear has always worn the mask of holiness.

The Knife by the Bed

The night of the screams will never leave me. That sound - raw, guttural, inhuman - ripped through the last of my compassion. The knife glinted under the lamplight like punctuation at the end of a long sentence.

That was when survival overrode empathy.

When I ran, barefoot, calling my friend, calling the cops, I wasn't just fleeing him, I was fleeing the version of myself that still believed she could save him.

The nervous system's final mercy is clarity through crisis. When threat reaches its peak, illusion dies instantly.

Detention as Divine Intervention

Watching him get cuffed, crying, pleading "Babe, please help me," was surreal.

For a moment, I felt pity, not for him, but for humanity's endless cycle of cause and denial. He thought consequence was persecution. But consequence isn't cruelty; it's correction.

Neuro-ethical realism reframes this as homeostatic morality: systems self-correct through breakdown when coherence is breached too long.

His detention wasn't punishment; it was data. The field had closed the circuit.

The Abortion and the Aftermath

When the ultrasound showed faint heartbeat, high risk, low chance, I knew.

The body was giving me permission to end what the mind already knew was unsustainable. That decision wasn't murder; it was mercy - for me, for the child, for the field that deserved peace.

When it was done, I felt no divine wrath, only silence. Not empty silence, restorative silence. The kind that follows truth finally acted upon.

Guilt came later, not because I'd sinned, but because culture said I must. But guilt fades when replaced with understanding. The body forgives faster than religion ever will.

The Neuro-Ethical Lesson

    1. Faith without inquiry breeds delusion.

    2. Love without boundaries breeds dependency.

    3. Empathy without discernment breeds danger.

I had lived all three.

And the synthesis of them became my philosophy: morality is not obedience; it's biological alignment with coherence.

Closing Reflection - The Descent into Duality

Every time I doubted myself, I was standing at the edge of awakening. Duality isn't the enemy, it's the teacher. It shows you every lie you've swallowed and dares you to spit it out.

When belief and biology finally reconcile, you stop confusing suffering with purpose. You start choosing peace without needing permission.

And that's how descent becomes ascent, not by climbing out, but by understanding what the fall was for.

CHAPTER 9

The Return to Reason

I used to think reason was what you used after chaos.
Now I know it's what chaos trains you for.

When Mum announced she wanted to buy a house
overseas, I told myself this was my chance to reset; help
her, get away, breathe. But leaving one battlefield
doesn't mean the war is over. Your nervous system
packs light; it takes the memories, not the luggage.

The Pilgrimage of Obligation

Helping Mum was muscle memory. I said yes before
thinking. Every daughter who's lived in guilt knows that
reflex - the body's automatic response to duty. I told
myself I was doing the decent thing. But decency
without boundaries is just exhaustion in moral clothing.

Neuro-ethically, that's learned self-erasure: when
empathy overrides agency. It masquerades as goodness,
but it's just fear rehearsing politeness.

The Cycle of Helping and Hurting

Mum and I clashed, patched things up, repeated. We were two nervous systems fluent in each other's triggers. She wanted control; I wanted peace. Both of us mistook regulation for love.

When she nagged about my smoking, my clothes, my silence, it wasn't about cigarettes or skirts. It was about her anxiety seeking order through me, and when I snapped back, it wasn't rebellion, it was my biology fighting for oxygen.

That's the thing about generational trauma: it doesn't need to be believed to be obeyed.

Foreign Land, Familiar Patterns

Overseas, nothing went to plan. No taps, no lights, no toilets; just chaos wrapped in bureaucracy. I realized stress sounds the same in every language.

I tried to laugh it off. Mum called it a test from God; I called it bad project management. Either way, it taught me this: faith that ignores logistics isn't spirituality, it's avoidance.

Moral Arithmetic: Helping vs. Healing

For months I built a house that wasn't mine, for a woman who still thought I was a disappointment. That's when I discovered a hard truth; helping people who refuse growth is self-harm in disguise.

The nervous system records that contradiction as pain. It's why burnout feels like heartbreak; they're biologically identical. Both are signals that coherence has been compromised.

The Return and the Relapse

When I came back to Melbourne, I promised myself peace. Instead, I found my ex still living in the house I'd bled to rent. He said he'd stay downstairs. He said he was "broken." He always said the right things - sorrow as currency. And I, professional empath, accepted every cheque.

That's when I coined my own internal term: the Pity Loop. It's when compassion forgets accountability and keeps feeding the same hungry ghost. I stayed out of fatigue, not forgiveness.

Serial Dependence and Emotional Debt

He sat beside me in the garage, chain-smoking, lamenting his misfortunes. I nodded, exhaled, sympathized, not because I believed him, but because I was conditioned to soothe discomfort.

We confuse comfort with control, and pity with peace.

That's how abusers rebuild access; through shared sorrow.

Neuro-ethical realism calls this mirror sedation: when empathy numbs instead of heals.

Rotating Roofs and Restless Souls

When my brothers took turns housing me, I felt like luggage labelled fragile but inconvenient. I scrubbed floors, cooked meals, paid in gratitude. They meant well, but every gesture reminded me that stability was still something I borrowed, not owned.

Reason started whispering then:

"Freedom isn't found; it's built from boundaries."

The Ghost in the Phone

Online dating felt like window-shopping for possibility. But every profile carried the same pattern - men seeking mirrors, not minds. Each conversation was another rehearsal of trust versus instinct.

When one of them vanished without explanation, I didn't chase closure. Instead, I studied the data.

Absence is information.

That's reason; the point where emotion finally stops editorializing reality.

The Temple of Hypocrisy

The divorce hearing - or what religion called reconciliation through elders - was the theatre of male control at its peak. They made me justify freedom like a criminal applying for parole. Four men, pens in hand, weighing my worth against scripture.

They called it faith.

I called it feudalism with better stationery.

That's when neuro-ethical realism crystallized: morality outsourced to hierarchy becomes abuse.

True conscience doesn't require witnesses.

Cultural Parasites and the Price of Purity

My sister-in-law meant well, but her coaching turned femininity into strategy.

"Be softer," she said. "Be slower to reply."

Translation: mute your authenticity, amplify his ego. That's how women get domesticated - not through violence, but through etiquette. Every "wait three hours before you reply" is a micro-betrayal of the self.

Reason began taking notes.

When Status Replaces Substance

The plumber with the ring - the recycled ring - was another sermon in symbolism.

I wasn't angry about the jewellery; I was angry at the metaphor. How many women before me had accepted someone else's leftovers just to prove they were "lucky"?

Reason whispered again:

"You don't need to be chosen; you need to choose."

Ghosting and the Lesson of Absence

When he vanished, my grief wasn't over him; it was over the illusion that decency guarantees reciprocity. Empaths often mistake effort for worth. But relationships aren't graded by moral attendance, they're graded by mutual coherence.

That week of silent tears was my emotional detox.

Every sob was a neuron recalibrating to truth.

The Neuro-Ethics of Rumour and Reputation

When rumours surfaced at work - that I was "easy" - I laughed first, then cried later. Because deep down, I knew what it really meant: women with autonomy are threats in cultures that worship compliance.

That's why gossip exists; to police those who no longer participate in their own oppression. It's the social nervous system's way of attacking healthy cells.

Reason told me: you can't argue with infection; you can only outgrow it.

The Field of Solitude

Fitzroy was my rehab.

From its high windows, I watched strangers who didn't know my name. For the first time in decades, anonymity felt holy.

I worked, trained, saved, smoked less, smiled more. The quiet was medicinal.

This was the nervous system's recovery phase - still scarred, but functional.

Still human.

That's the biological signature of healing: not perfection, but predictability. The ability to wake up without dread.

Closing Reflection - The Return to Reason

Reason isn't sterile; it's sacred.

It's the state of conscience that arrives after the nervous system has finally finished screaming. I once thought my life was a series of bad choices. Now I see it as an experiment in pattern recognition; a moral PhD written in cortisol and courage.

The data is clear:

Every repetition was an opportunity for recalibration.

Every heartbreak a stress test for integrity.

And when the dust finally settled, the lesson stood simple and unshakable: conscience is not a voice from heaven, it's the nervous system choosing coherence over chaos.

CHAPTER 10

The Descent of Control

I once believed danger came with warning signs, shouting, slammed doors, a clear sense of threat.

Now I know control arrives dressed as care.

When I met him, I was the healthiest I'd ever been; early-morning gym sessions, clear skin, clean lungs, and a full heart. I'd built a body that could carry its own peace, and that, ironically, was the body he sought to own.

He didn't come waving red flags; he came speaking my language - equality, respect, open-mindedness. The voice of a man who'd "been through it." My nervous system mistook familiarity for safety; my empathy mistook pain for proof.

The Mirage of the Healed Man

He told me about his trauma like it was a résumé of suffering: the violent father, the mother who "provoked" him, the sister he "protected," the abuse he endured. I saw a survivor. But trauma doesn't always produce empathy; sometimes it produces imitation.

When I listened, my body softened. I remember the ache in my chest; the reflex to soothe. That's the first signal neuro-ethical realism teaches us to read: when compassion overrides caution, you're already negotiating with danger.

The Switch

He walked into my home like a story I already knew - polite, spiritual, charming, broken.

That night, when he crossed the line without consent, I froze. The body's oldest survival algorithm - the collapse response.

He whispered after, "It's fine, we're meant to be."

Predators often use language to rewrite trauma into intimacy. It's a neurological hijack: they replace your perception of violation with a script of belonging.

I told myself it wasn't rape because he smiled after.

That's how moral systems fracture; when the body knows one thing and the conscience hasn't caught up yet.

The First Trade

When he told me to quit my job, my relief outweighed my logic. He'd "protect" me, he said. "I'll cover the rent if things get tight." It felt like partnership; it was actually procurement.

The neuro-ethical mistake here wasn't trust, it was delegating agency.

When you let someone else manage your stability, you teach your nervous system dependence disguised as devotion.

The Currency of Care

He called it equality, but he meant obedience. Every receipt he kept, every "rule" disguised as fairness, was an audit of my autonomy.

He said: "A good wife listens."

I heard: A safe woman submits.

Control masquerading as culture isn't tradition, it's tyranny written in familiar handwriting.

The Breakdown of Meaning

I wanted to believe in partnership, so I rationalized every cruelty:

his contempt for women, his obsession with money, his mother-hatred, his God-of-cash sermons.

He wasn't religious, he was ritualistic about dominance.

He wasn't looking for love; he was looking for compliance that smiled back.

The ethical lesson here isn't "avoid men like him."

It's "study the system that taught you to redeem men like him."

When Empathy Becomes Entrapment

I excused his anger as trauma.

I told my children, "He's unwell."

I turned bruises into metaphors for patience.

That's the neuro-ethical paradox of compassion: the same circuitry that fuels moral repair also fuels moral self-destruction when it ignores evidence.

Every time I soothed him, my nervous system was recording a moral inversion, mercy for the abuser, guilt for the victim.

The Strangulation Scene

The night he almost killed me is not just a memory, it's a data point.

In neuro-ethical realism, we call this the collapse threshold: the moment the body's survival instincts override belief systems.

When his hands closed around my neck, I wasn't just losing oxygen; I was losing doctrine; religion, culture, forgiveness, all gone in a few seconds of pure biological clarity, and that's when I understood something my upbringing never taught me:

God doesn't test your endurance of abuse. He tests your ability to leave it.

The Aftermath

He apologized the next morning, coffee in hand, eyes soft. That's how abusers reset the cycle: they offer gentleness not as atonement, but as sedation. Forgiveness became my coping mechanism; it also became his weapon.

He called my tears "beautiful."

That's when I realized: for him, empathy was entertainment.

The Daughter's Mirror

When he hit my daughter, time froze. Her face - blood, disbelief, and betrayal - became the reflection of every woman before us who'd mistaken endurance for virtue.

That moment split me in half: mother and philosopher.

As a mother, I wanted to protect her.

As a philosopher, I saw the neuro-ethical root of generational trauma: when obedience is rewarded and resistance is punished, morality becomes mimicry.

My daughter's silence after wasn't weakness; it was the body protecting coherence when safety is unavailable.

The Theology of Power

When he declared, "The only God is the God of money," I saw the full anatomy of his delusion.

For him, power was divine, control was sacred, and women were collateral.

That sentence ended my spiritual confusion. I realized faith without ethics is fanaticism; religion without empathy is theatre.

Neuro-ethical realism calls this the moral dislocation: when ideology severs itself from embodied conscience.

You can't argue theology with a nervous system trained for conquest.

Survival as Philosophy

By the time I started hiding money, pretending to agree, and smiling to stay alive, I was no longer a wife, I was a behavioural scientist conducting field research inside hell.

I observed his cycles, logged his triggers, tracked his tone. Survival turned analytical. My morality wasn't naïve anymore; it was strategic.

That's when the theory of neuro-ethical realism was born: the understanding that conscience isn't abstract; it's chemical, reactive, and adaptive.

When coherence is under siege, the brain rewrites morality into tactics.

The Final Lesson

He called me beautiful one more time, right before another assault, and in that instant, beauty became my camouflage, the mask that let me gather strength unseen.

To outsiders, I was compliant.

Internally, I was calculating my exit plan, my next breath, my next paycheck, my next act of quiet rebellion.

When you live in terror long enough, clarity becomes your religion. Every neuron, every gut twist, every tremor becomes scripture.

That's what Neuro-Ethical Realism ultimately teaches: morality isn't a rulebook; it's a survival algorithm evolving towards coherence.

And the first commandment of that algorithm is simple: "Do not let love talk you out of reason."

CHAPTER 11

The Collapse of Coherence

Birth is supposed to be the body's most sacred act; proof of creation, of continuity, of life expanding. But when you're living under coercion, birth becomes the moment biology itself rebels.

I'd gained thirty kilos, my pelvis felt like splintered glass, and my back threatened to snap. Each contraction was an argument between survival and surrender. And still, he came to me for sex, invoking God as his permission slip. Religion had turned my body into public property, a terrain for entitlement disguised as duty.

That's where coherence begins to fracture, when belief demands the body's silence.

The Body as Battlefield

I lay there, nauseous and immobile, trying to turn with a pillow between my legs just to stop my pelvis from grinding.

He didn't stop. "A wife must provide," he said.

The pain blurred into disbelief, not just in him, but in everything I'd been taught about submission, love, faith.

That's the moment conscience becomes physical. Not a whisper in the mind, but a tightening in the gut, a pulse of revolt under the ribs.

Morality begins in the tissues long before it becomes theology.

Cytomegalovirus and the Collapse of Control

When the doctor said, "You've contracted CMV," I didn't process it as illness. I heard it as verdict. Something foreign had infiltrated my body; a mirror of the man beside me, the faith around me, the entire structure of control I'd been breathing for years.

Every cell seemed to shout, Get him out. Get it all out.

That's the neuro-ethical signal of collapse: the body translating emotional violation into biological rebellion.

The Birth

Labour began with machinery, monitors, the hiss of gas, the sound of my own voice breaking. He left to go to the bathroom right before the final push. By the time he came back, there was blood, life, and the sound of nurses yelling instructions, and I was gone somewhere between consciousness and instinct.

When he finally spoke, his words were an infection worse than CMV:

"You let a man touch you," he said, furious that the nurse who stitched me was transgender.

In that single moment, every illusion collapsed. I wasn't married to a man; I was chained to a system, and the system had no interest in women surviving, only in them submitting.

The Largest Baby on the Ward

He weighed nearly 6 kilos. Everyone marvelled. The nurses smiled; he scowled.

He loved that my body could produce something strong but hated that it had required his absence to do it.

That's the contradiction at the heart of patriarchy: worship what you own, destroy what you can't control.

Recovery as Resistance

After discharge, the body tried to heal while the environment stayed toxic. I learned the art of strategic compliance, agreeing outwardly while plotting internally. I smiled to avoid explosions. I whispered gratitude while stashing cash.

Every deception was a moral experiment: how to preserve coherence in captivity.

That's what neuro-ethical realism teaches: when truth becomes dangerous, silence becomes strategy, not surrender.

The Drive

When he refused to put his name on the birth certificate, I understood it wasn't about money, it was about erasure.

To deny paternity was to deny accountability. It's the same trick every manipulator uses - remove the evidence, rewrite the narrative, weaponize doubt.

So, I confronted him.

And the car became a cage.

When his fist smashed into my face, I didn't think, I'm being assaulted. I thought, so this is coherence breaking.

The body knew before the brain did: this wasn't love, this was entropy.

The Collapse

He screamed, spat, hit, then suddenly became calm - the predator's rhythm.

When the police came, I lied. "I fainted," I said. That lie was my survival algorithm: protect the children, protect the plan, live to strategize another day.

And that's where the philosophical pivot happens - morality and survival aren't opposites; they're sequential stages of consciousness. You can't be moral in captivity. You can only survive until you're free enough to be moral again.

The Morning After

He brought me hot chocolate like nothing happened. A ritual apology, a saccharine reset. He quoted scripture about angels cursing wives who go to bed angry.

That's when faith became absurd to me, not because I lost belief in God, but because I finally saw how men rebranded guilt as piety.

The Sentence That Froze My Blood

"When we're good, I love him. When we're bad, I want to kill him."

He said it about our son. That's when the body's moral intelligence went into overdrive - the ache behind the sternum, the nausea, the hyperawareness of danger.

That wasn't fear; it was data.

The conscience is a biofeedback system; it reports reality in sensations when reason is still in denial.

The Visit to His Father

His father, frail and stained from neglect, offered us his savings. I declined. Control isn't cured by money; it's funded by it, and when I said no, I saw the flicker in Boo's eyes, that old wound of entitlement tearing again.

To him, love was ownership; to me, love was freedom. That's the unbridgeable gap between belief and biology.

The Sleepless Months

Bub's cries were symphonies of exhaustion. My daughter helped, bless her, still a child herself. But when I asked him to take one night, he snapped - light switch punched, eyes burning, the performance of rage.

That was the night I accepted that he'd never change because control had become his coherence.

If he ever lost dominance, he'd collapse completely.

The Prayer That Changed Frequency

I stopped praying for him to change. I started praying for strength to leave, and that's when divinity stopped sounding like doctrine and started feeling like data - as if God was a nervous system too, recalibrating toward coherence.

Closing Reflection - The Collapse of Coherence

Every woman who's lived through terror knows this moment: the quiet, post-violence awareness that nothing external can save you.

The body becomes oracle.

The nerves become scripture.

And the lesson reads simple but unflinching: when coherence collapses, morality doesn't die, it evolves into survival.

That's where Neuro-Ethical Realism is born - in the space where belief breaks and biology begins to speak.

CHAPTER 12

The Reconstruction of Self

People imagine freedom as a door you walk through. But for those who've lived inside control, freedom starts smaller - as a question whispered through exhaustion:

"What if I'm not the one who's broken?"

That question is the first sign of reconstruction. It's the nervous system testing the perimeter of the cage.

The Marriage Counsellor Experiment

When he agreed to counselling, I already knew what I was doing; it wasn't hope, it was reconnaissance. I wanted to see how an external moral authority would decode him. Every abuser fears a witness with credentials.

He walked in confident, ready to charm. He walked out furious.

The counsellor had seen straight through him, diagramming the "cycle of violence" as though reading my diary aloud. He'd told the truth about hitting me and showed no remorse.

That's when I learned a neuro-ethical law of survival: guilt and remorse are not twins. Guilt belongs to conscience; remorse belongs to ego.

He had one, not the other.

The House of Control

At home, every day was a new test of containment. He'd flirt with women, praise strangers, and weaponize silence with me. Then he'd talk about marriage, not as union, but as contract; not to heal, but to reclaim.

Control wears many faces, but its voice is always the same: "You owe me."

He said he wanted to make things official; I knew he wanted access to my income. That's when I began storing cash. It wasn't just money, it was oxygen in paper form.

Empathy Fatigue

By the end, I wasn't angry, I was neurologically depleted.

Empaths hit burnout not from cruelty, but from explaining reality to people committed to denying it. I wasn't in love; I was studying behaviour.

And that's how conscience evolves - it stops romanticizing pain and starts analyzing it.

The Fracture Point

When he bit my son's arm at the dinner table, the line between fear and fury snapped.

It's one thing to harm me, another to harm my child. Every maternal nerve fired like a siren.

That's when instinct and morality became indistinguishable, a single command pulsing through the bloodstream:

Leave.

The Exodus Algorithm

That night, I planned our escape. No melodrama, no tears, just logistics.

I packed while pretending to tidy, smiled while cataloguing threats, spoke softly to avoid triggering suspicion. That's how women in captivity become tacticians - philosophers in aprons, generals in disguise.

Neuro-ethically, this is adaptive morality - conscience morphing into strategy.

The Police, the Proof, the Pattern

When the counsellor and later the police confirmed what I already knew, something inside me stabilized.

I wasn't crazy. I wasn't dramatic. I was accurate.

Accuracy is the first stage of recovery. Truth stops being emotional and becomes statistical:

He hit me.

He threatened me.

He endangered my children.

That's not narrative, that's evidence.

The Illusion of Reform

After the arrest came the apologies. Soft voice. Religious phrases. "I'm not myself."

It's the classic neurological bait: guilt as hypnosis.

But I'd begun decoding him. His contrition had rhythm, not depth. Real remorse disrupts the pattern. Performative remorse preserves it.

The Psychology of Debt

He said, "I gave you that money."

I said, "Then here, take it back."

He refused.

That's when I saw what it really was - a psychological lien, a chain disguised as generosity.

To repay it wasn't about finance; it was about moral sovereignty.

You can't heal while indebted to your oppressor.

The Predator's Religion

He quoted scripture as camouflage. In his mouth, God became a legal defense, not a moral compass. He used faith to reset the hierarchy - man above woman, silence above truth.

That's not religion; that's ritualized narcissism.

Neuro-ethical realism calls this spiritual inversion: when belief serves biology's hunger for power instead of conscience's hunger for coherence.

The False Peace and the Second Collapse

For a while, the texts softened. "I miss you." "We can work it out." Then came the manipulative empathy:

"I'm sick. Help me. You're the only one who understands."

Predators recycle compassion like a renewable energy source. I fell for it one last time, not out of love, but fatigue.

Empaths relapse through mercy.

The Car Attack

The day he tried to run me down, everything slowed to data. Tire marks, trajectory, intent. My driver yelled out; I stayed still.

That's how survival rewires the brain - panic becomes precision.

Later, at the police station, when I replayed the voicemail where he said he'd kill me, I didn't shake.

The body had become analyst, not victim.

That's the final transformation of conscience under trauma: the nervous system becomes the witness.

Aftermath: The AVO and the Apartment

He got an AVO - 500 metres. Distance measured in law, not in healing. But when I shut the apartment door that first night, I felt something I hadn't in years: predictability.

It wasn't happiness. It was the absence of chaos, the baseline from which conscience can rebuild.

That's when I realized: peace isn't the opposite of violence. It's the nervous system returning to reason.

Sex, Recovery, and the Ethics of Want

When I went back on the dating app, it wasn't rebellion; it was recalibration. After being objectified for years, I wanted to choose the object for once. No fantasy, no forever, just agency.

To outsiders, that sounds reckless.

But for survivors, controlled pleasure is the antidote to coerced pain.

Desire reclaimed is morality re-owned.

Therapy and the Rebuild

My psychologist didn't ask for a confession. She gave me diagrams, the same ones the counsellor used to warn me. This time, I studied them without panic.

Patterns. Triggers. Recovery loops.

That's how moral intelligence grows, through repetition until recognition becomes reflex.

At the gym, every rep felt like a prayer to coherence. Weights grounded me better than sermons ever had. Discipline replaced chaos. Sweat became scripture.

Closing Reflection - The Reconstruction of Self

The reconstruction of self isn't about forgetting; it's about re-filing. Pain moves from story to study. Love moves from sacrifice to standard, and conscience stops whispering and starts instructing.

I stopped asking why me and started asking how does this happen, because only through comprehension does survival become philosophy. So now, when people ask what Neuro-Ethical Realism means, I tell them this:

It means your morality is only as free as your nervous system is safe.

It means forgiveness is useless without boundaries.

And it means that every survivor who still tells the truth - calmly, coherently, repeatedly - is already a philosopher of the highest order.

CHAPTER 13

The Retrieval of Power

When you've lived inside distortion long enough, truth stops being emotional, it becomes procedural.

You don't scream it anymore; you document it.

You don't beg to be believed; you file evidence.

That's how the reclamation begins, not with rage, but with records.

The 32-Page Truth

I built my case like a reconstruction of sanity.

Thirty-two pages - screenshots, messages, photos - not to convince anyone I was right, but to prove, to myself, that I hadn't imagined any of it. He'd made me delete our entire message history the week after I left, pretending it was to "move on." He was erasing evidence while rehearsing innocence.

That's how manipulators operate: they weaponize remorse as data collection.

By decoding his patterns, I was performing my own kind of neuro-ethical surgery - extracting infection from memory.

Every sentence I typed was an act of moral calibration.

Facts instead of feelings.

Logic instead of longing.

The nervous system was finally writing its own affidavit.

The Aunt's House

Even his family began to fracture around his lies. His aunt, once loyal, saw through him - how he twisted compassion into control. In her living room, as he unravelled under her questions, I realized that moral recognition doesn't come from bloodlines; it comes from biology - from those who can still feel.

He had lost that ability. His conscience was anesthetized.

That's the essence of neuro-ethical realism: morality is a physiological skill. Lose empathy long enough, and you lose the ability to perceive truth.

Systemic Shackles

The court became a mirror of my old captivity - slow, bureaucratic, male-patterned in its apathy. I wasn't in danger anymore, but I was still being processed. I learnt quickly: the system protects order, not people.

I wasn't pleading now; I was auditing - tracking correspondence, noting contradictions, becoming fluent in procedure. It was exhausting, but precision became my armour. The more coherent my evidence, the less his chaos mattered.

That's the new morality: coherence as defense.

Meeting the Rational Man

Then came him, the man I called Stallion.

At first, he was just a pause, a breath between hearings. Then he became the reintroduction of reason. He didn't talk in riddles, didn't project, didn't demand reverence. He debated ideas, not identities.

For a mind recovering from gaslighting, logic feels like oxygen.

He spoke of ethics without religion, of responsibility without domination. It was the first time conversation itself felt moral, not performative, not coercive, just reciprocal.

When he sent a heater to keep my kids warm, it wasn't charity, it was coherence in action.

That's the difference between rescuers and partners: rescuers offer control, partners offer stability.

Safety as Philosophy

For months, I waited for the mask to drop - the critique, the withdrawal, the test.

It didn't.

Instead, he stayed steady. He was proof that power and gentleness aren't opposites; they're competencies of the same moral nervous system.

Through him, I realized that the human conscience operates like muscle memory: once trained by harm, it flinches even at safety. But with consistency, it learns again; tension releases, awareness resets, trust becomes tolerable.

The Conversation of Transparency

When I told him my story, I was braced for recoil.

Instead, he listened like a researcher, not dissecting, not diagnosing, just receiving. He said, "You've learnt through pain. That's not shameful; it's education."

That's what separates moral maturity from moral vanity: the former integrates pain; the latter hides it.

In that moment, I understood the neuro-ethical definition of trust: the willingness to stay coherent in front of another person's truth.

The System's Blind Spots

The legal processes dragged on, each affidavit another labyrinth of jargon. Even my solicitor seemed numbed by repetition.

The family law machine doesn't differentiate between victims and manipulators, only between those who can afford to persist and those who can't. I couldn't relocate; the system had shackled me geographically in the name of "stability."

But moral stability isn't about location. It's about autonomy; the freedom to make coherent choices without retaliation. So, I built it myself - spreadsheets, folders, contingency plans - all quiet revolutions of order.

The Return of Logic

Each court form, each call to the police, each affidavit corrected another internal imbalance. For years, I'd been gaslighted into emotional chaos. Now, structure itself was therapy.

I didn't want vengeance; I wanted equilibrium.

That's what recovery really is - coherence restored.

The Proposal

When Stallion proposed, it wasn't the ring that moved me, it was the timing. It happened amid hearings, affidavits, and subpoenas.

He was reminding me that love isn't the opposite of struggle; it's the infrastructure that holds you steady through it. His steadiness became the new metric of morality; reliability as the highest form of love.

Biology of Safety

My headaches began to ease. My breathing slowed again. That's the body confirming what the mind already knew - coherence isn't abstract; it's physiological.

Peace isn't just an emotion; it's a measurable state of the nervous system when reality finally aligns with ethics.

I watched my children sleep without the hyper-vigilance that once haunted every night.

That's when I realized: my recovery wasn't just psychological; it was ethical homeostasis.

Closing Reflection - The Retrieval of Power

Power doesn't return as dominance. It returns as discernment. It's the quiet confidence that no one can rewrite your history again.

So, when I think back on those 32 pages, the screenshots, the affidavits, the ring, and the hearings, I see them all as part of the same process: the nervous system reconstructing its moral architecture.

Truth, when recorded calmly, is the highest form of rebellion, and coherence, not forgiveness, is what sets you free.

CHAPTER 14

The Return to Coherence

Healing isn't a straight line, it's a recalibration. After trauma, even joy feels suspicious. Peace feels temporary. You learn to scan every quiet moment for the next explosion.

That's how recovery begins, not through serenity, but through vigilance slowly unlearning itself.

The Shared House

When Stallion and I moved into that run-down 1940s house, it wasn't just a place to live; it was a lab for moral rehabilitation.

The kitchen was falling apart, but it didn't matter. We were testing something bigger - whether two people with trauma could share air without contaminating it with fear.

He worked as a cook, I juggled courts and babies, and the nights blurred into survival with a hint of tenderness.

For the first time in years, someone stayed.

That's when I realized that coherence doesn't mean calm, it means consistency.

The Marriage of Intention

We married quietly, papers signed, lunch shared, nothing ornate. After everything, I didn't need witnesses; I needed truth.

It wasn't romance I craved, it was a moral equilibrium, someone whose presence didn't distort my perception of reality.

The wedding didn't sanctify us; stability did.

The Courts Again

When Boo walked free with a community order, celebrating like he'd won a prize, something inside me detached completely.

Justice wasn't blind, it was bureaucratic.

The law didn't feel moral; it felt mechanical.

That's when Neuro-Ethical Realism became more than theory. I understood: the system can only measure behaviour, never conscience.

You can't legislate empathy.

The Quiet Man

Stallion didn't preach. He didn't perform guilt. He just showed up, calm, capable, grounded. He didn't compete with my pain, he absorbed it.

That's how I knew he wasn't part of the old pattern.

The truly healed don't demand forgiveness; they embody reliability.

I studied him like data - how he argued, how he paused, how he repaired, and for the first time, I didn't feel the need to defend my intuition.

The Fracture Between Faith and Control

I'd seen too many men use God as a weapon. Scripture had become theatre for tyranny. But when Stallion spoke of faith, it wasn't about control, it was about ethics.

His spirituality wasn't performative; it was behavioural.

That's the dividing line between religion and realism: faith should enhance conscience, not replace it.

The Law Degree

When I enrolled in law, it wasn't ambition, it was retaliation against helplessness. Every statute I studied, every case I dissected, was an attempt to reverse the imbalance of power.

Law became my exorcism. But it was also exhausting; trauma doesn't respect timetables or exams. My mind was brilliant and broken at once.

At night, I'd rock in my chair, staring at the printouts I couldn't process, my nervous system looping through the residue of courtrooms past.

And yet, I persisted.

That's the difference between coping and evolving; one maintains function; the other rewrites code.

The Mirror of Stallion

While I crumbled, he sought therapy.

While I doubted, he studied healing videos, journaling quietly beside me.

Without realizing it, he was teaching me the male version of coherence - structure without dominance.

We were re-parenting each other's nervous systems.

The Second Descent

Stress returned as insomnia, guilt, and arguments.

Every time he went back to Melbourne for his kids, I felt the old panic of abandonment. My body didn't care that he was good; it only remembered that gone meant danger. That's the paradox of recovery, trust feels unsafe at first.

Wine numbed the noise. For a few hours each night, I stopped analyzing every sound in the house, every vibration in my chest.

It wasn't addiction; it was anesthetic.

The system needed downtime, even if it came in liquid form.

The Light of Purpose

Then one night, Stallion looked at me and said, "You should write your story."

I laughed, half horrified, half flattered.

But when he said, "You could help others understand survival," something ancient in me stirred.

It wasn't vanity. It was duty. Maybe the pain wasn't pointless after all.

That was the conception of *Trial by Trust*.

And though I didn't know it yet, it would become the fieldwork for Neuro-Ethical Realism itself.

The Family and the System

The courts kept rewarding the man who weaponized faith. Reports came back "positive." Judges prioritized procedure over pattern recognition.

It was like watching empathy get litigated out of existence.

That's when I understood, systems can't heal what they refuse to feel.

The Return of Logic

I threw myself back into work as a dental nurse. It was ordinary, repetitive, grounding, exactly what I needed. Healing hides in routine, in sterilized trays, clean surfaces, and predictable outcomes.

After years of chaos, predictability was divine.

CHAPTER 15

Shrapnel - The Ethics of Recovery

Healing is never total. You carry fragments - invisible metal lodged in tissue. Every stress, every smell, every memory that hits too close reminds you: the war may be over, but the body still flinches.

The Marathon

I was functioning on fumes - studies, court, parenting, money, trauma. Life wasn't linear; it was concurrent chaos. Some nights I told Stallion he could leave if it got too heavy.

He refused every time.

That's when I realized: stability is proven in repetition. Every "I'm not going anywhere" re-wired a neuron that once believed everyone would.

Neuro-Ethical Integration

We both stopped smoking, then over-corrected with wine, tattoos, pets, and adrenaline. We weren't reckless; we were re-sensitizing. After numbness, sensation feels like resurrection.

Every piercing, every puppy, every laugh was rebellion against despair. The nervous system heals not through perfection, but through participation.

The Seed of Purpose

When Stallion urged me to write, he wasn't just suggesting therapy, he was prompting moral evolution. He saw that my story wasn't just personal; it was systemic evidence.

He said, "People need to see what it takes to stay human."

And he was right.

That's the essence of Neuro-Ethical Realism: turning lived experience into moral data for others to decode.

The Recurrence of Control

Meanwhile, the courts rewarded my abuser again.

"Positive reports." "Extended access."

Those words should have felt fair; they felt fatal. Systems mistake compliance for cooperation. They confuse politeness with peace.

That's why so many survivors look calm in court, not because they're healed, but because they're disciplined.

The Children and Their Choices

My daughter's relationship with a man like Boo was my worst déjà vu.

Watching it unfold, I had to restrain the rescuer in me; you can't save someone mid-lesson. Morality can't be inherited; it must be chosen.

Even my sons' paths mirrored the push and pull of independence - one seeking escape, one clinging to stability.

That's what generational coherence looks like in progress - chaotic, imperfect, evolving.

The Diagnosis

When the headaches became unbearable, I demanded an MRI. A one-millimetre aneurysm, tiny, yet symbolic. The physical manifestation of years of pressure. Doctors said it wasn't the cause of the pain. Maybe they were right; maybe the pain was ethical, not anatomical.

The brain stores conscience like a hard drive; overload it with contradiction long enough, and something gives.

The Shift to Criminology

I left law, not in defeat, but evolution. I didn't want to interpret the system anymore; I wanted to understand why people break it.

Criminology gave me language for pathology, not procedure.

That's the next stage of recovery - curiosity replacing victimhood.

The Puppies and the Paradox

When our dogs had puppies, I cried after rehoming them.

Not because I lost them, but because for once, I had the power to choose when to let go.

That's healing: controlled endings.

Closing Reflection - The Return to Coherence

Coherence isn't perfection, it's the ability to return to self after disruption.

I still had shrapnel in me - scars, triggers, memory loops - but they no longer dictated my direction. They were reference points, not anchors.

Healing isn't the absence of pain. It's the presence of perspective.

And as I began to write *Trial by Trust*, I realized that the story wasn't just about what I survived, it was about what I understood through surviving.

That's the final law of Neuro-Ethical Realism: when you translate pain into pattern, you reclaim authorship of reality itself.

CHAPTER 16

The Moral Horizon

There comes a point when the fight stops being about survival and starts being about definition.

You stop asking, Why me? and begin asking, What does this reveal about us?

That's the moment of ethical awakening; when personal suffering becomes data for collective evolution.

The Body in the Witness Stand

When I stood in the courtroom, trembling through the oath, my conscience was not abstract, it was cellular.

My jaw locked, pulse surged, and breath fractured. My entire body became an instrument of testimony before I even spoke.

That is what trauma does; it rewires honesty into reflex.

The Justice's eyes met mine with rare empathy, and for a moment, my body calmed enough to find words.

That pause was morality in action; an unspoken acknowledgement of shared humanity amid procedure.

Four years of hearings, affidavits, and contradictions later, I finally understood the irony: Justice may live in law, but conscience lives in flesh.

And while the system measures words, the nervous system measures truth.

The Ethics of Exhaustion

When the judgment came - sole responsibility granted, visitation supervised - I didn't feel victory; I felt depletion.

Ethical endurance has no trophies. It is measured in nights without sleep, migraines without cause, and the quiet ability to still get up and cook breakfast for a child who needs normalcy.

Each legal form I filed was an act of neuro-ethical realism in motion; biology regulating morality through repetition and documentation.

Provocation and Proof

His messages returned - polite, then taunting, then cruel.

Screenshots became survival.

In a just world, empathy would suffice. In this one, metadata is protection.

Every new text, every antagonizing emoji, proved what philosophy alone cannot: that immorality is not ignorance, it is intention without empathy.

He wasn't confused. He was calculated.

So, I documented everything - not as obsession, but as coherence.

To record is to refuse distortion.

The Sharp Instrument

When my son reported that his Dad pierced his skin, time collapsed.

The sharp sting on his leg became the embodiment of every invisible wound I had tried to expose. My heart raced, skin flushed; biology's alarm bells sounding the same as moral outrage.

That moment crystallized my theory: ethics is sensory first, cognitive second. We feel wrongness before we can name it.

The police dismissed us. Systems always prefer data without discomfort.

But I had already seen enough to know: the body knows the truth, even when the law refuses to listen.

Systemic Fatigue

Legal Aid. Rejections. Contraventions. Bonds.

It wasn't bureaucracy anymore; it was moral decay disguised as order. I wasn't just tired; I was ethically hypoxic - suffocating from years of being told to prove what was already lived.

When the verdict punished me for protecting my child, something in me went quiet. I realized that justice, like faith, is only sacred if it can feel pain.

The Biology of Defiance

I turned to movement - boxing, Muay Thai, sweat, breath, grit.

Every punch was a moral recalibration. Each drop of sweat rewrote my nervous system's narrative from submission to sovereignty.

My trainer didn't see a victim; she saw voltage; the human body remembering its own power.

That's what healing looks like under Neuro-Ethical Realism: action as philosophy. Movement as morality.

The Spiral of Systems

Even as the courts failed, something new awakened.

I began decoding patterns - how institutions mirror abusers: demand compliance, punish emotion, reward silence.

It's not coincidence; it's structure.

And once you see it, you can't unsee it.

The system wasn't built for coherence; it was built for control.

So, I decided to stop expecting empathy from architecture.

Instead, I began designing my own ethical infrastructure - boundaries, records, rest, training, writing, and truth.

The Move

Moving back to Melbourne felt like repatriation, not to geography, but to self. When Boo claimed he'd moved too, I laughed.

Because now I knew: proximity doesn't equal power.

Every kilometre I drove south was another layer of fear shedding. By the time I crossed the border, I was carrying exhaustion, yes, but also an evolved conscience: one that no longer needed validation from either courts or clergy.

The Return of the Sons and Daughters

My children's lives unfolded like case studies in inherited resilience.

One battled cycle of coercion, another of compassion fatigue, all learning, painfully, the same neuro-ethical law: that morality without autonomy is just obedience.

I guided, not controlled.

Advised, not indoctrinated.

Because parenting, under this new realism, isn't ownership, it's mentorship in moral biology.

Revelation

Then came vindication: the Ombudsman's report confirming I had been misrepresented.

It wasn't revenge, it was equilibrium restored. Validation not as ego, but as evidence that the universe tilts toward coherence when you persist long enough.

Closing Reflection -The Moral Horizon

At the edge of survival, philosophy finally became lived truth.

Neuro-Ethical Realism was never an idea; it was my body's defense mechanism intellectualized.

I had become proof that biology and morality are one continuum: cells carrying conscience; nerves translating truth.

When the courts quietened and the messages stopped landing, I realized; this wasn't peace by circumstance; it was peace by calibration.

The moral horizon is not a place you reach. It's the moment your biology and ethics finally agree on what you will no longer tolerate.

EPILOGUE

The Age of Self-Authorship

I am no longer the student of systems; I am their critic.

No longer the subject of indoctrination; I am its counterexample.

The End of Obedience

I was raised to equate obedience with goodness. Now I see that unquestioned obedience is the death of conscience.

Every act of dissent was a neurological correction; my brain re-mapping itself from compliance to critical thought.

Religion gave me ritual; trauma gave me evidence.

Philosophy gave me freedom.

Inheritance Rewritten

My home is no longer ruled by doctrine or fear. My daughter's freedom is not rebellion, it's repair. My sons are being raised not as saviours, but as sovereign beings; men whose masculinity is defined by empathy, not control.

That is what the next generation deserves: moral autonomy encoded from the start.

Faith Without Fear

Religion taught me honour but also submission.

Now I honour the divine by questioning it.

If God exists, surely, He prefers honesty over obedience.

That's my creed now: truth is the highest form of worship.

Legacy of Logic

Every woman silenced in the name of purity becomes a philosopher the moment she asks why.

Every survivor of coercion becomes an ethicist the moment she chooses coherence over conformity.

That's the new enlightenment; not the one in books, but the one in nervous systems recalibrated by truth.

Closing Invocation

I am not broken.

I am the data of everything that survived.

I am biology learning how to tell the truth out loud.

To lawmakers, I say:

Listen. Feel. Redefine justice through empathy.

Because laws without biology will always fail the human body.

And to every woman still inside the system, whispering her story into the void:

You are not the problem. You are the prototype of moral evolution.

The Age of Self-Authorship begins here.

No gods. No abusers. No false authorities.

Just the biology of conscience finally standing upright, and saying, without apology:

"I am human.

I am coherent.

I am free."

After the Noise

I've told my story twice now.

Once as pain, and once as pattern.

The first book was a pulse - raw, honest, human.

This one is the echo that learned how to steady that pulse and make meaning from it.

When I began writing *Trial by Trust*, I didn't know what healing looked like.

I only knew what survival felt like.

But now, after walking through every memory, theory, and quiet night of questioning, I know this much - healing isn't about forgetting the noise; it's about tuning it into signal.

I used to think conscience was something moral people had, and broken people lost.

Now I know it's the opposite.

Conscience is what breaks first, and what rebuilds truer, if you let it.

Every scar becomes a nervous system note that teaches you what peace should sound like.

This book isn't the end of that learning. It's a record of the moment I decided that my biology, not my past, gets to define my truth.

It's proof that philosophy doesn't need a classroom; it just needs courage.

To those still caught between who they were and who they're trying to be,

trust the quiet.

It's your body remembering the direction home.

And to everyone who ever told me to tone it down, stay polite, be grateful -

thank you.

You taught me that my defiance was data. That every "too much" was a sign of how accurately I felt the world.

If you've read this far, you already carry the same capacity -

to sense truth, to turn ache into alignment.

So, take these pages, fold them into your own life,

and when someone asks where you learned your strength,

tell them it was never learned.

It was remembered.

Because conscience doesn't live in theory, it lives in the body that survived.

www.ingramcontent.com/pod-product-compliance
Lightning Source LLC
Chambersburg PA
CBHW060519290526
45791CB00001B/453